THE GOI

OSLO
AND SURROUNDINGS

THE CITY AND ITS MONUMENTS, ARCHITECTURE, MUSEUMS, PORT, ART, AND NATURE

BONECHI

Aune

Aune Forlag AS
Lade Alle 63
7041 Trondheim
Norway

Publication created and designed by: *Casa Editrice Bonechi* - Editorial Management: *Monica Bonechi*
Graphic design: *Monica Bonechi* - Layout, make-up and cover: *Manuela Ranfagni*
Text: *Patrizia Fabbri* - Editing: *Patrizia Fabbri* - Translation: *Paula E. Boomsliter* - Drawings and maps: *Stefano Benini*
Drawing page 94, bottom: *Tryqve Lindeberg AS* (courtesy of *Casa Editrice Perseus Plurigraf*)

© Copyright 2008
Casa Editrice Bonechi, Via Cairoli 18/b – Florence – Italy
email: bonechi@bonechi.it

Printed in Italy by *Centro Stampa Editoriale Bonechi*.

The photographs used in this publication are property of the *Casa Editrice Bonechi* archives and were taken by
Marco Bonechi and *Andrea Fantauzzo* (pages 92 bottom, 93, 94 bottom left, 95).

Other photo contributors:
Samfoto, Oslo: pages 6 top (*Bård Løken/Samfoto*), 6 bottom (*Espen Bratlie/Samfoto*),
8/9 (*Svein Grønvold/Samfoto*), 15 top (*Bjørn Rørslett/NN/Samfoto*), 15 bottom (*Fredrik Naumann/Samfoto*),
34 (*Fredrik Naumann/Samfoto*), 44 top right (*Bård Løken/NN/Samfoto*), 89 (*Espen Bratlie/Samfoto*);
Photo Scala, Florence: page 44 top left and bottom.

Photographs pages 4 top, 6 center, 7, 10/11, 18 bottom, 20/21 bottom, 23 bottom, 25, 31 top, 33 bottom, 36, 37,
38/39, 52, 58/59 bottom, 60 top and bottom left, 66 bottom center, 67 top, 81 top left and bottom left, 83, 84-87,
88, 90/91, 92 top (*photos Ole Petter Rørvik*); 55 top (*photo Giulio Bolognesi*); 35, 51 bottom (*photos Scanpix, Oslo*);
9 top (*photo Urpo A. Tarnanen, Oslo*): courtesy of *Aune Forlag, Trondheim*.

Photographs pages 45 (*photo Ufficio Nazionale Norvegese per il Turismo di Milano*),
94 top (*photo Tine Kjøkken/Ragge Strand*), 94 bottom right (*photo Opplysningskontoret for Kjøtt*):
courtesy of *Casa Editrice Perseus Plurigraf*.

The publisher apologizes for any unintentional omissions and would be pleased to include appropriate
acknowledgements in any subsequent edition of this publication if advised by copyright holders.

ISBN 978-88-476-2297-5
www.bonechi.com

INTRODUCTION

Oslo, the capital of Norway, is set in an extraordinarily beautiful landscape at the head of the Oslofjord, surrounded by forest-mantled hills. In the time of the Vikings, the site was occupied by a small trading center called Viken. Oslo as such was founded about 1050; in 1624 it was entirely destroyed by a mammoth fire. King Christian IV built a new city on the site and called it Christiania; the name endured until 1924, when the capital once again took its ancient name.

Oslo is a paradise in both summer and winter; its cultural life is on a par with any great capital; and it is an eminently livable city. Today, the recently-inaugurated Opera House is a spectacular new accent on the city skyline and an exceptional classical entertainment venue. But Oslo also sports a surprising number of cafés and clubs featuring various types of musical entertainment, jazz first and foremost. There are many restaurants, where you'll find both typical Norwegian cooking and the best of international cuisine, and a great number of art galleries and museums: the Kon-Tiki Museum, the Viking Ship Museum, and the celebrated Munch Museum, to name just a few. And don't forget a visit to the unique Vigeland Park.

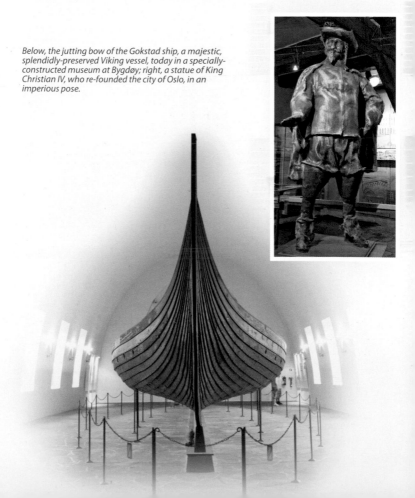

Below, the jutting bow of the Gokstad ship, a majestic, splendidly-preserved Viking vessel, today in a specially-constructed museum at Bygdøy; right, a statue of King Christian IV, who re-founded the city of Oslo, in an imperious pose.

The deep, enchanting Oslofjord, crisscrossed day and night by boats, ships, and ferries. Just outside of the port of Oslo, the vessels hug the coast of the Bygdøy peninsula, famous worldwide for its waterfront museums.

THE FIORD

The deep Oslofjord is full of small islands (40 within the city limits), many of them served by the ferries that depart almost continually from the port behind City Hall. Summer, the finest season for the fiord, is the perfect time to enjoy watersports and the sun on one of the islands and swim in the waters of the fiord—or in one of the many lakes around the city; for example, Sognsvann. We might even say that the Oslofjord, 100 kilometers in length from the Færder lighthouse to the capital, is Norway's premier venue for free-time activities.

THE VIKINGS

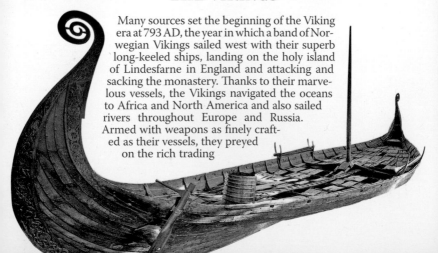

Many sources set the beginning of the Viking era at 793 AD, the year in which a band of Norwegian Vikings sailed west with their superb long-keeled ships, landing on the holy island of Lindesfarne in England and attacking and sacking the monastery. Thanks to their marvelous vessels, the Vikings navigated the oceans to Africa and North America and also sailed rivers throughout Europe and Russia. Armed with weapons as finely crafted as their vessels, they preyed on the rich trading

centers of the Mediterranean and Russia, penetrating as far as Constantinople (today's Istanbul), capital of the great Byzantine/East Roman empire. Archaeological digs in Norway have brought to light remains of Viking ships that have been fully reconstructed after having lain buried for more than a thousand years. But the Vikings were not just warriors and aggressors; they were also accomplished traders and they created well-organized kingdoms founded in law and justice. Their extensive mercantile activities demanded that they establish ports for embarking and debarking goods; this is how Norway's first cities were born: Oslo, Trondheim, and Tønsberg. With their simple lifestyle and pagan religion, the Vikings' society may be defined as primitive—yet their civilization was the foundation of a great culture.

Top, an extremely ancient Viking helmet of spectacle-like design, on display Historical Museum. The Viking regulars generally wore a conical helmet in iron and probably leather, with wood and iron reinforcements, while the captains were protected by an iron bowl with a nose guard or full face mask and a chain mail curtain protecting the neck and nape.
On these pages: elaborately-decorated Viking ships, still fully fitted down to their oars, that suggest all the fascinating complexity of a civilization that was, at once, primitive and very much at the technological avant-garde. The combination of tradition and modernity that made Oslo's history is still a touchstone in development of the Norwegian capital.

Winter in Oslo is snow, ice, light, and color, despite the long winter nights. And open-air sports, from cross-country skiing to skating and spectacular acrobatics on the stage of the world-famous Holmenkollen ski-jump, in the immediate environs of the capital.

WINTER IN OSLO

Winter is a magical season in Oslo, where the attractions go well beyond the ice-bound waters, the snows, and the long, northern nights. Instead, winter is synonymous with color and Oslo's long night with revelry in the innumerable pubs and bars as well as in the typical restaurants. And as the Christmas season approaches, the atmosphere becomes even more beguiling. From the city center, it's just a short ride on the Holmenkollbanen metro line to the famous ski jump, to enjoy the panorama of the city from observation deck on high. Less well known, but no less exciting, are the more than 2600 kilometers of cross-country ski trails that wind through the area, in a fabulous natural setting, some lighted for night-time skiing. And after a satisfying day on the snow, the city is waiting with its myriad opportunities for an evening of pure relaxation.

Oslo in the Third Millennium
The New Opera House

Oslo is not only a livable city, abounding in green areas and attractions: it is also a city that has always aimed at ensuring a high quality of life and has demonstrated a singular capacity to push to the avant-garde in art, architecture, and modern technology while respecting the environment and tradition. Constant, never-ceasing progress has resulted in construction of quite a number of new buildings, complexes, and centers in the Norwegian capital, all of modern conception yet perfectly integrated in a context of rare natural beauty between the blue waters of the fiord and the green hills that crown the hollow in which Oslo lies. As part of this ambitious urban development plan, Oslo inaugurated its new Opera House (*Operahuset*) on the bank of the fiord in the Bjoervika district of the city center on 12 April 2008, with a gala celebration including extraordinary concerts and performances. The huge cultural building, designed by the architects of the Norwegian Snøhetta studio to serve as the new home of the Norwegian National Opera and its celebrated corps du ballet, makes ample use of white marble cladding that emphasizes the clean, essential lines of the structure.

Sprawling over an area of 38,500 m², with more than 100 rooms and concert and performance halls of all sizes, the futuristic building is already a point of reference in the industrial port area. The white roofs of the "iceberg" that slopes into the fiord are open to visitors for an unforgettable stroll and a never-to-be-forgotten vista over the fjord and the harbor area.

An image gallery of the spectacular new Opera House that dominates the waters of the Oslofjord with its unmistakable profile. Note, in particular, the extraordinary architectural lines that characterize the futuristic building and the vast, sculpted roof surfaces, accessible to visitors. The structure was inaugurated on 12 April 2008 with a solemn ceremony and a stunning fireworks display.

FIRST ITINERARY - THE WATERFRONT

City Hall - Nobel Peace Center - The Port - Aker Brygge - Ibsen Museum

In the very center of Oslo, in the western sector of its urban tapestry, directly overlooking the port's crowded wharves, a relatively modern district has progressively emerged as the new heart of the Norwegian capital. It is here that the mighty City Hall soars above the skyline, here that the most disparate activities are concentrated in a frenetic flurry; and this is the point of departure for the fast ferries to Bygdøy, Oslo's green peninsula famous for its recreational facilities and its museums, including the unique Viking Ship Museum.

Unmistakable with its monumental form, its numerous Modernist statues (including a representation of Saint Hallvard, patron of Oslo, leaning outward from the facade), and the enchanting east tower clock, the largest in Europe of this type, the massive City Hall dominates the port and the cityscape. Here, the south facade.

RÅDHUSET
(City Hall)

A city with a millenary history, Oslo has today elected a modern, Modernist monument as its symbol: the imposing City Hall, faced in distinctive, rigorously handmade brown brick, which dominates the busy port with its massive twin towers and fortress-like central portion, was named Oslo's "structure of the century" in 2005. The building, with its strong architectural personality, was designed by Arnstein Arneberg and Magnus Poulsson. Construction began in 1931 but, given the forced interruption of work decreed by World War II, was terminated only in 1950—in time, however, to be inaugurated on occasion of the nine-hundredth anniversary of the city's birth.
In the interior, in the many, splendidly-appointed ceremonial halls,

Its every element a celebration of Norwegian history, culture, and society, the Oslo City Hall is adorned with statues illustrating the most disparate workaday activities, occupations, crafts, and professions. Facing page: top, the Munch Room; bottom, the Rådhushallen during a Nobel Prize award ceremony.

Pages 16-17: The south facade of City Hall, looking out over the port, and the main facade on the north side (in the inset), facing the city, where the complex clock, decorated the twelve signs of the zodiac, takes pride of place.

artists of world renown vied to create the "acres" of marvelous wall decorations. For example, an entire wall in the vast *Rådhushallen* (or Main Hall, where every year since 1990, on December 10th, the Nobel Peace Prize award ceremony has been held) is covered by Europe's largest oil-on-canvas, an area upwards of 1500 m^2 on which Henrik Sørensen, fêting Norwegian society, painted *The Norwegian People at Work and in Celebration*; the *Munch Room* is home to *Life*, an important painting by the artist for whom the room is named; the luminous *Banquet Room* (*Bankettsalen*) stands out for its elegant decorative ornamentation; and the no less impressive *Festival Gallery* boasts an elaborate fresco by Axel Revold, who offers the viewer a minutely-detailed representation of Norwegian society in the mid-20th century, subdivided into its different economic sectors: agriculture, industry, fishing, and—only naturally—shipbuilding.

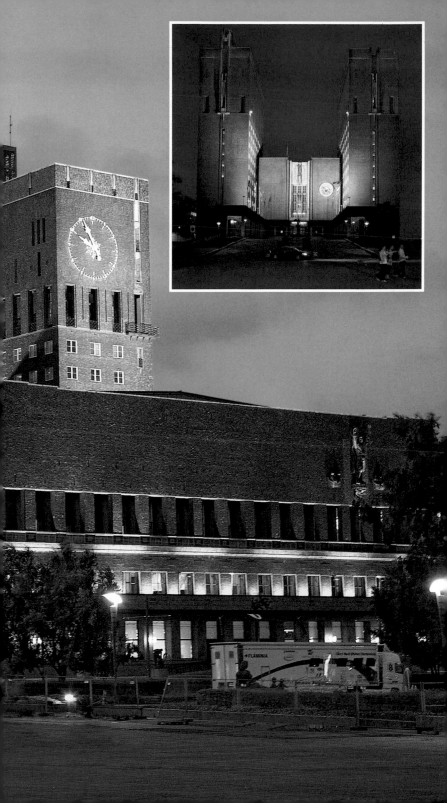

The new, elegant home of Oslo's Nobel Peace Center was originally a simple railway station.

NOBELS FREDSSENTER
(Nobel Peace Center)

Just a short distance from City Hall, an old railway station has been restructured, to plans by David Adjaye, and since 2005 has been the elegant seat of the fecund and extremely active Nobel Peace Center. The center, it's true, houses an interesting museum, but it is also much more: here, besides "meeting" all the Nobel laureates through history, visitors may participate in a constructive ongoing discussion of themes pertinent to world peace, war, and the various conflicts that afflict the world today, a debate animated by permanent exhibitions, conferences, films, and avant-garde interactive technologies, including a huge electronic newspaper dedicated to the work of the Nobel Peace Prize winners. Another "must" is a visit to the harmonious, suggestive *Nobel Garden.* Inspired by Norway's rural tradition of cultivated rooftops, the project, titled "Self-Sustainable Garden," represents an ideal world in the spirit of Alfred Nobel, where technology, ecology, and tradition all work together within a practical architectural system.

The Peace Medal

The medal awarded to Nobel Peace Prize laureates, a replica of which adorns the facade of the Nobels Fredssenter, is solid gold and carries a portrait of Alfred Nobel. It was designed by the celebrated Norwegian sculptor Gustav Vigeland.

Modern technologies, extraordinarily suggestive presentations, film clips, and photographic exhibits all make important contributions to perpetuating debate centering on the complex and always topical subject of world peace and the thousand conflicts that still rage across our planet.

THE PORT OF OSLO

A part of the area around City Hall, on the banks of the deep fiord, is taken up by the industrious wharves of the city's great port, free of ice year-round and for this reason one of northern Europe's most active cargo and passenger gateways. From here depart the ferries to the *Bygdøy* peninsula and others that ply the waters of the *Oslofjord* on unforgettable excursions; here both tourist yachts and freighters tie up; and here, in the warm season, the many fishing boats just in from the North Sea offer their fresh catch for sale on the jetties and their crews prepare an exquisite delicacy: red shrimp (*reker*) blanched on the spot to be eaten hot from the pot.

The great port of Oslo is a haven for vessels of all types, from ferries to motorboats, to fishing boats, to huge freighters.

Views of Aker Brygge, a short distance from Oslo's City Hall, on the west side of the port, where revamped industrial buildings host a modern commercial and entertainment center with extraordinary architectural, historic, and cultural value.

AKER BRYGGE

One of Oslo's most popular districts, *Aker Brygge* is perhaps one of the best examples of what the urban redevelopment program that has changed the face of the Norwegian capital has succeeded in attaining. Here, west of today's City Hall area, beyond the new silhou-

ette of the Nobel Peace Center, the *Akers Mekaniske Verksted* ship-yards began their activity in 1857. When the shipyards were closed in 1982, the problem of what to do with the buildings was immediately addressed. A vast architectural requalification program, launched in 1986, resulted in creation of a veritable small city, crowded with shops, department stores, apartments, offices, movie houses, a theater, restaurants, pubs, discothèques, and open-air meeting places, all behind a dock that can accommodate small vessels. The happy union of futuristic architectural solutions and historic functional structures thus gave form to a structure that today can rightly be considered one of Oslo's principal attractions, a shopping and entertainment center where, above all in summer, the city's cultural and night life is

The jetties and wharves of the Port of Oslo, and therefore also of Aker Brygge, with its brick buildings, are always crowded with sailing and fishing boats, commercial vessels, and the ferryboats that offer vital transportation services—for example to the nearby Bygdøy and its museums—but also excursions and cruises. And just as busy are the pubs and eating places offering cool drinks and local gastronomic specialties. On many of the fishing boats, instead, you'll find the typical red shrimp boiled up by the crew—a finger-scorching taste treat (bottom right).

concentrated, an authentic pole of attraction for the young and not-so-young, who crowd the piers and wharves and the quais with their enticing outdoor seating and floating bars. Five thousand people live and work here; here you'll find music and dancing—and it's a great place just to stroll and enjoy to the full the splendid, bright Scandinavian summer nights.

Striking modern exhibits in the public area of the Ibsen Museum.

IBSENMUSEET
(Ibsen Museum)

Born in 1828 in Skien, in southern Norway, the dramatist Henrik Ibsen is considered the greatest Norwegian author of all times. And yet, despite a precipitous success that resulted in his being named art director of the Norwegian Theater of Christiana, as Oslo was then known, in 1857, Ibsen moved abroad in 1863 and sojourned in Austria, Denmark, Germany, and Italy until 1892. His most famous works, from *A Doll's House* to *Ghosts*, were penned during this period. Ibsen was in his sixties when he finally decided to return to his homeland, where an apartment in Oslo, just a stone's throw from the Karl Johans Gate and the Royal Palace, became his and his wife Suzannah's last home. After 1895 the apartment became his "den" in more than one sense; it was here that he created his last works and then spent the last years of his life as a shut-in, afflicted by a terminal

Ibsenmuseet

illness that resulted in his death in 1906. The apartment, restored in 2006 on occasion of the hundredth commemoration of Ibsen's death, hosts an interesting **museum** dedicated to the great dramatist's life and work. It is divided in into two sectors, one open to the public, with permanent and itinerant exhibits, and another, in what was once the Ibsens' private rooms and which is open for guided tours, where everything, from furnishings to fixtures and wall coverings, is absolutely faithful to the original: even the colors have been retouched and are the same as they were in Ibsen's time.

More images of the Ibsen Museum, with its original references to the dramatist's artistic production and, right, a photographic portrait of the famous playwright.

Ibsenmuseet

II itinerary - Karl Johans Gate

Royal Palace - Karl Johan Avenue - National Theater - University -
National Gallery - Historical Museum - Parliament -
Cathedral - Central Station

Historical
Museum, page 46

Parkveien

Slottsparken

Det Kongelige Slott

St. Olays gate

Hist.
museet

Nasjonal-
galleriet

Universitetet

Kristian IV's g

Nobelinstituttet

Drammenveien

Nationaltheatret

Karl Johans gate

Royal Palace,
page 32

SELØKKA

Munkedamsvelen

Stortingsgata

Cort Adelers gate

Konserthuset

Fridtjof
Nansens
plass

Rådhuset

National Theater, page 42

Rådhus
plass

Rådhusgata

Akersgata

Akershuskaia

Kongensgate

Karl Johan Avenue, page 36

Parliament, page 51

A long, straight thoroughfare runs from east to west through the heart of Oslo, linking the Royal Palace with the Central Station: Karl Johans Gate. All around, an elegant district with much luxuriant greenery, where the principal points of reference for the city's political and social life coalesce.

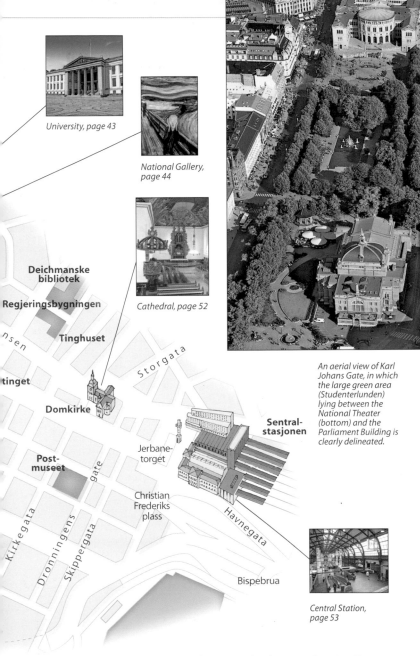

University, page 43

National Gallery, page 44

Cathedral, page 52

Deichmanske bibliotek

Regjeringsbygningen

nsen

Tinghuset

tinget

Domkirke

Storgata

Post-museet

gate

Jerbane-torget

Christian Frederiks plass

Kirkegata

Dronningens

Skippergata

Sentral-stasjonen

Havnegata

Bispebrua

An aerial view of Karl Johans Gate, in which the large green area (Studenterlunden) lying between the National Theater (bottom) and the Parliament Building is clearly delineated.

Central Station, page 53

When in 1818 the Marshal of France Charles Jean-Baptiste Bernadotte, designated heir to Charles XIII by the Swedish parliament, donned the united crowns of Sweden and Norway as Karl XIV Johan (Karl III Johan in Norway), one of his first concerns was to improve his second capital, Oslo. It is no wonder, then, that one of the city's most interesting and prestigious areas is still clearly linked to him in name and history.

Images of the majestic facade of the Oslo's Royal Palace, in front of which the Royal Guard parades (bottom right). When the king is in residence, a gold lion on a red ground flies from the flagstaff over the entrance.

DET KONGELIGE SLOTT
(Royal Palace)

When he became king of Sweden and Norway, Karl XIV Johan proceeded to equip Oslo, like his Swedish capital, with a residence "fit for a king" and the capital of a country. He thus turned to Hans Ditlev Franciscus von Linstow, one of the premier architects of the time (who was later involved in laying out the area that would become the Karl Johans Gate district), and charged him with designing a three-story palace in an elevated, dominating position at the start of the great boulevard, as the home of the king whenever his duties bought him to Norway. The year was 1818. From conception to completion, the project spanned three decades, during which there progressively emerged a dignified building with essential, regular lines surrounded by a vast park (*Slottsparken*) that is today open to the public. The complex work of decorating the interiors, which are still outstanding in terms of the refinement and polish of their ornamentation, in a variety of styles, began in 1836. Peter Frederik Wergmann was the author of the friezes in Pompeiian style that embellish the walls of the great *Banqueting Hall*; von Linstow—who wanted a vestibule in rigorously Norwegian Classicist style and a dining hall inlaid with vibrant, brightly-colored decorations inspired by the frescoes of Pom-

The equestrian monument to King Karl XIV Johan by Brynjulf Bergslien (1875) which imperiously dominates the vast plaza in front of the royal residence.

peii—took a personal interest in the decoration of the immense *Ballroom*, (360 m² surface area with 10.7 meter ceilings) and the *Palace Chapel*, whose altar was erected over the foundation stone of the palace; with eminently National Romantic feeling, Johannes Flintoe frescoed the unique *Bird Room* with a true and truly impressive hymn to the natural assets and history of Norway. Unfortunately, Karl XIV Johan died in 1844 and did not live to see his residence completed. The new Royal Palace was thus officially inaugurated by Karl's son and successor, Oscar I, in the fall of 1849. King Oscar, however, lived in the palace for only brief periods in connection with his official duties, and in a relatively short time the structure began to show signs of serious degradation. Only with the ascension to the throne of Haakon VII, who with his wife Maud was the first ruler to inhabit the palace on a permanent basis, did the destiny of the residence drastically change. The subject of repeated restoration, renovation, and modernization efforts (the latest, massive, rehabilitation

Two images of the interiors of the Royal Palace. Top, the refined Red Drawing Room, furnished with sober sophistication; bottom, the grandly appointed yet restrained Council Chamber.

campaign was conducted in the late 20th century), embellished and continually inhabited by the royal family since Haakon's time, the palace has finally taken its rightful place as a true point of reference in the life of the city and the country. Today, the Royal Palace is open for guided tours during the summer months and has also offered the public the occasion to view its vast collection of works of art. What is more, on May 17th, Norway's Constitution Day (National Day), tradition leads a crowd of celebrants accompanied by music and costumed, flag-waving children to assemble in the vast square in front of the palace (*Slottsplassen*) around the *equestrian statue of Karl XIV*, to acclaim the royal family, which responds to the salutation from the balcony. And every day, at 1:30 p.m., the same square is the venue for the flamboyant ceremony of the *Changing of the Guard*.

THE ROYAL FAMILY

The history of the Norwegian monarchy reaches a thousand years into the past, even though it comprises precise and distinct parentheses in which the fate of the country was interwoven with those of Denmark (from 1381 to 1814), and Sweden (from 1814 to 1905). The current Norwegian royal family, especially well-loved and popular with their subjects, is of relatively recent—and Danish—origin. To succeed the Swedish King Oscar II on the throne of a Norway that in 1905 dissolved its personal union with Sweden and finally returned sovereign and independent, the Norwegian parliament selected the Danish Prince Carl, second son of Frederick VIII of Denmark and husband of the English Princess Maud of Wales, a granddaughter of Queen Victoria. With the name of Haakon VII, he was immediately hailed with enthusiasm by the population, which over time learned to appreciate his unpretentious but determined personality and his straightforward liberal politics. His firm opposition to Nazi-Fascism, which cost him an extended period of exile in England (1940-1945), only strengthened his prestige and confirmed his popular support. The same support that has accompanied his heirs, Olav V, who succeeded him in 1957, and Olav's son Harald V, Norway's current ruler, who ascended the throne in 1991. Harald is the first ruler of Norway to have been born on its soil in 567 years. With his wife Sonja and his two children (Crown Prince Haakon, heir-apparent, and Märtha Louise), he has further disposed the Norwegian monarchy toward all that is modern and has won great popularity among his subjects by bringing the institution closer to the hearts of the Norwegian people.

The royal family saluting the people: from left to right, Crown Prince Haakon holding his daughter Ingrid Alexandra, his wife Crown Princess Mette-Marit, Queen Sonja, and King Harald V.

Pullulating with bars, restaurants, and shops and dominated by the commanding facade of the Royal Palace, Karl Johans Gate, the Norwegians' favorite and busiest boulevard, always full of life, cuts through the heart of Oslo from east to west. Left, an image of the fountains in the Studenterlunden, the "Students' Garden" running alongside the thoroughfare.

KARL JOHANS GATE
(Karl Johan Avenue)

Another mid-19th century work springing from the creative flair of the architect von Linstow, ordered built by the king whose name it bears, Karl Johan Avenue (*Karl Johans Gate*) is undoubtedly the most famous and busiest boulevard in Oslo and indeed in all of Norway. It is a showcase for the Oslo that counts, traversed each day by thousands upon thousands of people, lined with neoclassical buildings and top-range shops, parks and gardens, bars and restaurants, and even a renowned skating rink. Dominated by the Royal Palace, which

On pages 38-39: the festive "Children's Parade" proceeds up Karl Johans Gate on 17 May of every year, in a sea of waving national flags, destination the Royal Palace. The National Day holiday, commemorating the signing of the Norwegian Constitution in 1814, is celebrated in all Norway's cities and by Norwegians abroad; in Oslo, it is also a great draw for tourists, who flock to the city to participate in the solemn yet fun-filled festivities.

sits solemnly at its western extremity, it is the address of the **Parliament** and the **University**, the **National Theater**, and the celebrated *Studenterlunden*, the "Students' Garden" with its sparkling fountains. At the other end of the boulevard from the Royal Palace is the *central railway station* and the picturesque *Kirkeristen Market*.

This wide, airy thoroughfare dotted with shop windows and open-air cafés is always crowded, always vibrant with life—even more so when it is the route of the "Children's Parade," accompanied by bands, that every year on 17 May marches to the Royal Palace to salute the king and his family on occasion of Norway's Constitution Day.

A pedestrian island in the portion between the Central Station and the Parliament Building, Karl Johans Gate is a true drawing-room boulevard, solemn and elegant, made even more suggestive by the lighting system installed in 2000 to provide fascinating nocturnal illumination for the facades of the flanking buildings.

NATIONALTHEATRET
(National Theater)

Preceded by the statues of Henrik Ibsen and Bjørnstjerne Bjørnson, the Norwegian poet who was Nobel Prize laureate in Literature in 1903 (and who numbers the verses of the national anthem among his works), an imperious facade surmounted by a pediment introduces the National Theater, the country's most important, inaugurated in 1899. One of the official opening performances was a work by Ibsen. Designed by Henrik Bull, built of brick, the prominent main theater building was damaged in 1980 by fire and underwent lengthy restoration. Today, it hosts the *Ibsen Festival* and is home to a significant *collection of paintings.*

The sober facade of the National Theater.

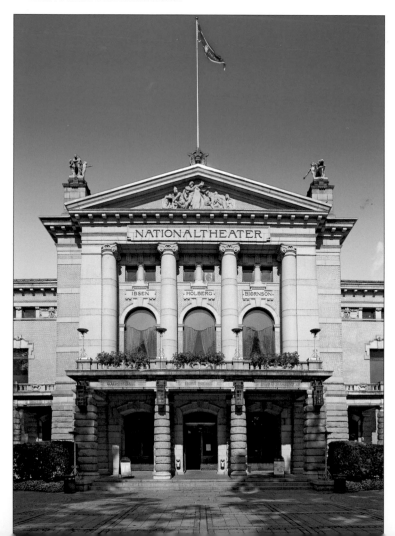

Top, the Old University. Right, the statue of the renowned poet Henrik Wergeland that seems to stand watch over the entrance to the Studenterlunden.

UNIVERSITETET
(University)

In 1811, King Frederick VI of Denmark decreed the founding of the first Norwegian university. When the university building was inaugurated, more than 40 years later (and by that time, by a Swedish king), the institution was nevertheless baptized "Universitas Regia Fredericiana" (*Det Kongelige Frederiks Universitet*). Today, many of the departments have been transferred to a new campus on the outskirts of Oslo, but the great neoclassical building is still a symbolic element on Karl Johans Gate and is especially well-known for its splendid auditorium, also known simply as the *Aula*. Built in 1911 and decorated with some of Edvard Munch's most spectacular frescoes (1916), until 1990 it was the venue for the Nobel Peace Prize award ceremony.

NASJONALGALLERIET
(National Gallery)

Founded in 1836 as an institution dedicated to the artistic production of the young Norwegian nation and today rightly considered the country's premier museum, the National Gallery boasts the world's largest collection of painting, sculpture, drawings, and engravings by Norwegian artists of all eras. The collection that took form over time highlights National Romanticism, Impressionism, and Modernism, and of course includes a section devoted exclusively to Edvard Munch's masterpieces.

For many years the collections had no permanent home; only in 1882 were they arranged in the building that still hosts the museum: a neo-Renaissance palace built especially for

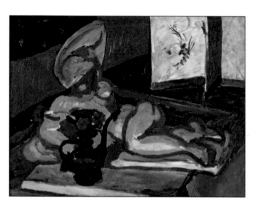

Facing page, the facade of the National Gallery. Among the most celebrated masterpieces here exhibited are certainly Henri Matisse's Sculpture and Persian Vase (1908, top left on facing page), and, by Edvard Munch, Horse Team (1919, left) and above all, The Scream (1893, above).

the purpose and since enlarged several times. Today, the 4,500 paintings, 900 sculptures, 17,300 drawings, and 25,000 engravings have been joined by the 50,000 volumes of the library devoted exclusively to art that is by now an integral part of the Gallery offer.

Nasjonalgalleriet

45

The Oslo Historical Museum illustrates the daily life, the art, and the crafts activities of the peoples that inhabited Norway from prehistoric times through the Middle Ages in accurate reconstructions living and working spaces (top) and its extraordinary collections (bottom left, ancient weapons and, right, an example of sacred art).

HISTORISK MUSEUM
(Historical Museum)

Considered the University museum, with its three original sections dedicated to national antiquities, medals and coins, and ethnography, the Historical Museum was founded in 1897. Today, it occupies the four floors of a modern building designed by Henrik Bull especially for the collections and inaugurated in 1904. With its extraordinary, prestigious collections, this great institution offers a sweep-

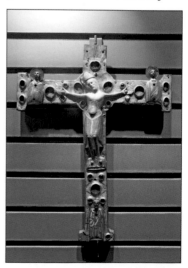

Historisk Museum

46

Top, an ancient bone comb. Right, the splendid portal from "Ål stave church", dating to 1150; it originally belonged to a very ancient wooden church, a type of construction that was widespread in the area at the time. With its original colors still partly intact and its sophisticated carving, it is one of the very few wooden objects from the medieval period still integrally preserved in Europe. Below, the room devoted to Norway's wooden churches.

Historisk Museum

47

ing panorama of Norwegian history—and more—from prehistoric times (and more precisely, about 9000 years ago) to our day, touching on an infinite variety of topics, from daily life to tradition and artisan and artistic production. In this perspective, especially interesting are the outstanding *Viking Age* collection, displaying the most conspicuous Viking treasure of gold in northern Europe, and *Medieval Art and Culture*, with an abundance of sacred objects and amazing wooden articles.

Facing page: several examples from the important collections displayed at the Historical Museum. In particular, a sarcophagus and a statue, two of the most precious items on exhibit in the ethnographic section devoted to Ancient Egypt. The mask at the bottom left, instead, is linked to the ancient magic rites of the Inuit culture of the Arctic regions. Bottom right, a well-known, very old Viking helmet. The leather clothing, the footwear, and the objects at the top of the page are also from the gelid Arctic.

On this page, one of the splendid, expressive wooden representations of the Virgin and Child, often still embellished with their original colors, that highlight the Sacred Art section and establish the extraordinary skill and great artistic flair of the 12th- and 13th-century Norwegian sculptors.

The major *ethnographic sections*, instead, explore the Far East, the Americas, and Ancient Egypt. And finally, another exhibit worthy of much more than a cursory glance: objects from the *Inuit culture*, a truly unique opportunity to discover the mysterious world of the Arctic.

Historisk Museum

Left, the Stortinget, seat of the Norwegian Parliament, with its refined interiors, welcomes 25,000 visitors each year.
Bottom, the King, flanked by the Crown Prince, presides over the solemn opening session of Parliament in October of each year.
Right, one of the characteristic statues that dot the Studenterlunden.

STORTINGET
(Parliament)

Designed by the Swede E. V. Langlet and inaugurated in 1866, the unmistakable, grandiose *Stortinget* building is home to the Norwegian Parliament. The legislative body of Norway is composed of two houses and counts a total of 169 members.

With its powerful bell tower, the Oslo Cathedral is the main feature on the square Stortorvet plaza. Bottom, the interior of the church with the ancient wooden pulpit and the splendidly-decorated ceiling.

OSLO DOMKIRKE
(Cathedral)

Consecrated in 1697, heavily refurbished during the course of the 19th century, and accurately restored in the 20th, the Oslo Cathedral, dedicated to Saint Hallvard, is the Norwegian capital's most important church, with 900 seats and a striking bell tower whose spire was added only in the 1800s.

The austere, severe exterior is belied by a luminous interior, essential yet splendiferous with decoration and Baroque furnishings. Besides the organ, the church's vaults include the ancient *wooden pulpit* and the elaborate *altarpiece*, of Dutch manufacture, both dating to the late 1600s and sculpted with acanthus leaves, and the *stained-glass windows* by Emanuel Vigeland, 20th-century works like the tempera ceiling paintings of *Scenes from the Old and New Testaments* by Hugo Louis Mohr (1936-1950). The cathedral again underwent restoration at the very beginning of the third millennium.

The plaza in front of the cathedral (*Stortorvet*), dominated by the 19th-century statue of King Christian IV, is the venue for Oslo's picturesque, brightly-colored flower market.

CENTRAL STATION

At the eastern end of Karl Johans Gate, on the spacious *Jerbanetorget*, a plaza overshadowed by the steel profile of the *Trafikanten Tower*, seat of a well-equipped public transport and tourist information office, we find Oslo's Central Station, a modern railway terminus from which it is possible to reach literally any point in the country on trains leaving almost non-stop. And right across the street, not far from the bus terminal and the metro stop, is the luminous, futuristic *Oslo City* shopping mall.

Right, the Trafikanten Tower. Bottom, the airy shopping gallery at Oslo's Central Station.

III Itinerary - Kvadraturen

Christiania Torv - Museum of the Norwegian Resistance -
Akershus Fortress - Akershus Castle

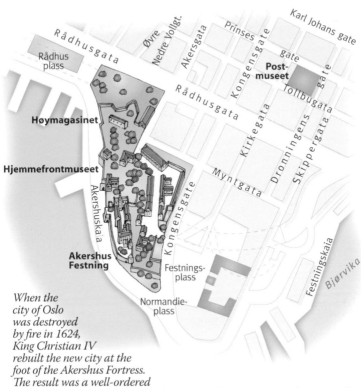

*When the
city of Oslo
was destroyed
by fire in 1624,
King Christian IV
rebuilt the new city at the
foot of the Akershus Fortress.
The result was a well-ordered
quadrilateral district with a grid layout and ancient houses that are still
the pride of the historic "Kvadraturen" district.*

Christiania Torv

What was once the market square of the reborn Christiania is still
lined with ancient, historic buildings—first among the many, the
Old City Hall, a 17th-century construction that is now home to the

Images of Christiania Torv. The beautifully-preserved historic buildings are still perfect complements even in Oslo's generally more modern architectural context and jewels in the setting of the ancient square, now the exclusive domain of pedestrians who delight in the typical restaurants and the cafés that offer the occasion to relax and enjoy a cup of coffee.
Bottom, the fountain that now defines what was once Oslo's market square, with the unmistakable statue symbolizing King Christian IV pointing to the site of his new city.

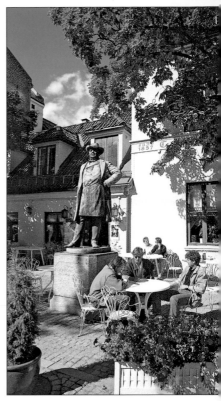

Theater Museum—which recent pedestrianization of the area has contributed significantly to valorizing. Another essential element in the new urban arrangement project for the square is the great fountain by Wenche Gulbrandsen, eloquently titled *The Glove of Christian IV*, that has stood in the square since it was restructured in 1997.

55

NORGES HJEMMEFRONTMUSEUM
(Museum of the Norwegian Resistance)

In the majestic fortified complex that opens out around the Akershus Slott, a dominant position is reserved for an ancient wood-and-stone building from the 17th century. Today, it is home to the Museum of the Norwegian Resistance, inaugurated in May 1970 on the 25th anniversary of the country's liberation. German troops reached Norway in April of 1940, and after subduing strenuous resistance in two months' time, began what can only be termed a ferocious occupation that lasted for five years. While King Haakon VII headed a government in exile from London, where the Crown Prince (later King Olav V) was born, the entire Norwegian population offered an example of great civic conscience, building a resistance movement that counted almost 50,000 fighters and conducted heroic actions that were anything but purely demonstrative. That extraordinary manifestation of civic civility under duress and national pride that was the Norwegian resistance is celebrated in this museum, where an extensive collection of documents, films, and recordings, united with a suggestive, extremely engaging exhibit layout, contributes to recreating the climate and the events that made Norwegian history during the World War II years. Near the museum, a *monument* recalls the many Norwegians who lost their lives during the devastating conflict.

The Bindingsverkshuset (literally, "Half-Wood House") is a characteristic 17th-century building inside the walls of the Akershus Fortress, in a commanding position over the Port of Oslo, that today is home to the Museum of the Norwegian Resistance.

Norges Hjemmefrontmuseum

Photographs, documents, posters, period objects, scale models, newspapers, recordings, film clips, weapons, accurate reconstructions, and an essential, highly-functional modern exhibition layout: everything in the Museum of the Norwegian Resistance serves to trace, recall, and document the five years of the terrible Nazi-Fascist occupation, from the invasion in April of 1940 to the liberation of Norway in May, 1945.

Norges Hjemmefrontmuseum

AKERSHUS FESTNING
(Akershus Fortress)

The great Akershus Fortress, with its massive bastions that rise protectively over the wharves and piers of the Port of Oslo, is one of the city's oldest buildings and most certainly one of the best-preserved of the historic structures. In 1299, King Haakon V ordered construction of a defensive bulwark to protect the important port and city of Oslo, named by him capital, from the heights of a rocky spur. In an age like the 14th century, when danger and ravaging sieges were a constant, the early fortified settlement became the most secure residence for the king's family and court. Damaged by repeated fires and then fallen into disuse, the fortress was finally adapted and partly rebuilt by Christian IV after the fire of 1624 that brought the entire city to its knees. The work carried out at that time gave the complex the form we still see today; the residential area was outfitted with elegant, spacious halls that today host state ceremonies and receptions, and the *Royal Chapel* was added. The chapel is the final resting place of many famous figures, including King Haakon VII and Queen Maud and

In two ancient arsenals inside the Akershus Fortress, the Armed Forces Museum (right) displays collections of weapons, uniforms, scale models, and interesting reconstructions. The especially rich and well-documented section dedicated to World War II features exhibits of torpedoes, underwater bombs, aircraft, and tanks, and places special emphasis on the naval and marine aspects of the conflict. Below, an overall view of the Fortress, its mighty bastions rising from the rocky point that juts over the Port of Oslo. A frequent guest of the port is an interesting full-rigged sailing ship built in 1937, the Christian Radich, *which owes much of her fame to the 1958 film* Windjammer.

King Olav V and his consort Märtha. The spaces that during World War II were the Nazi headquarters are now the home of the **Norwegian Armed Forces Museum**, depicting Norway's military and wartime history from Viking times to the 1950s.

Above, the south wing of the castle, with the spire of the Blue Tower rising behind the profile of the mighty building, with the vast, luminous Hall of Christian IV.

Facing page: with its ancient stone walls, narrow guard walks, bridges, and galleries, the exterior of the Castle remains brooding and austere.
Bottom right, the north wing overlooking the courtyard, which in the Middle Ages was divided into two parts by a tower destroyed in the fire of 1527. Today, elegantly reconstructed in Renaissance forms, it is dominated by two towers (in the photo, the soaring Romeriks Tower).

Akershus Castle
(Akershus Slott)

The fortunes and fame of Oslo's fortress are closely interwoven with the historic and epic military exploits of which it has been protagonist: over its long history, it was put to extenuating siege on nine occasions—yet it was never expunged. Particularly heroic was the 1716 resistance to the siege by the troops of Sweden's King Karl XII, who were unable to make so much as a dent in the impenetrable defensive bastions of the *Akershus Festning*.

But over the centuries, something quite different also took form within the insurmountable circle of walls: a spectacular royal residence, the Castle, which offered the royal family not only protection but also all the luxuries and amenities of a true royal palace. After the royal family first sought refuge inside its walls, the austere, essential structures of the medieval castle were expanded and adapted, becoming, by the mid-17th century, more rightly the spaces of an elegant Renaissance castle. The vast central courtyard was ringed by spacious halls embellished with precious decoration and fine furnishings, worthy of a ruler and his family, but without detracting in any manner from the defensive valence of the complex. Today, these perfectly-preserved, splendid halls offer venues for State ceremonies. During the summer season (but by reservation all year round) they are open for guided tours.

A visit to the Castle reserves quite a few pleasant surprises, like discovering the lovely *gardens* that open out within the bastions of the Fortress and the sightly outbuildings, once of strictly military destination but today finely restored. Also worth a visit is the spectacular *belvedere* from which an array of historic cannon looks out on the panorama of the city below. It is in this historic setting that the always inspiring spectacle of the *Changing of the Guard* takes place every day, punctually at 1:30 p.m.

Left, the Fortress walls from the south, with the cylindrical Munketårnet in the foreground.

The Interiors

The striking rooms of the Akershus Slott, the fortress of Oslo's Castle, represent a historic legacy of incredible beauty but also a cutaway of great documentary importance. Here, the details of everyday doings mix with history, art, and culture, communicating the values of a centuries-old civilization and modern philological recovery efforts.

Just a few examples. One of the first elements to attract the visitor's attention, in the south wing to the side of the Tower of the Virgin, is the solemn **Royal Mausoleum** designed by Arnstein Arneberg and completed in 1948 with precious marbles and the painting over the

Left, the solemn Royal Mausoleum, built in 1948 in correspondence to the Castle's chapel. The remains of King Haakon VII are preserved in the center white sarcophagus.

Right, the luminous Royal Chapel, simple and solemn at the same time, the only consecrated site on the Castle premises.

Top, the ancient Royal Archives wing (Fateburet), ordered built by Haakon V but destroyed by fire and rebuilt numerous times, in today's version, designed by Arnstein Arneberg in the 1930s. Above, original furnishings, figures in period costume, reconstructions of scenes and ambiences: thus the Castle of the Akershus Fortress returns to life in all its former splendor, projecting the visitor back through time to discover mysterious, far-off eras.

altar, a work by the Norwegian artist Henrik Sørensen. The mausoleum contains the broad white sarcophagus holding the remains of King Haakon VII, the Danish prince elected King of Norway in 1905 and deceased in 1957, and of his consort, Queen Maud, who died in 1938. Olav V (whose birth name, before he became Crown Prince of Norway, was Alexander), son of Haakon VII and Maud, instead lies since his death in 1991 in a green sarcophagus along-

Top, ancient weapons, utilitarian objects, and even splendidly colored tapestries like that shown above, depicting a lively scene from the Christiania of 1740, recall historic exploits as they enliven the solid, ancient walls in the Akershus Castle.

Bottom, the grandiose Hall of Christian IV in the south wing of the Castle, today used for official functions and in particular for State dinners.

side the remains of his wife, Märtha, a Swedish princess who died in 1954 before she could be crowned queen. In the building to the rear of the mausoleum is the vast, spectacular **Hall of Christian IV**, originally part of the ruler's apartments and subdivided into several rooms for the king's and queen's private use. Restructured and refurbished several times over the centuries, the space housed the Supreme Court (beginning in 1744), but after the disastrous collapse of the ceiling in the 1800s was converted into an arsenal. Extensive, accurate restoration during the 20th century lent the space its current majestic aspect, a single monumental hall made even more striking by the splendid 17th-century tapestries of the Flemish school, woven by Everaert Leyniers to cartoons by Jacob Jordaens and installed here in 1967.

Another extraordinarily prestigious space is without a doubt the **Hall of Olav** in the north wing; in this case as well, its current appearance is fruit of work conducted during the 1900s. The fact that

Top left, the striking Hall of Olav in the north wing of the Castle, with the distinctive wooden ceiling with exposed beams. The hall took the name of the then-reigning king, Olav V, when it was inaugurated after its restoration in 1976. Top right, the so-called Scribes' Room, once the workplace of the court administrators.

Bottom, a view of another room in the Castle, highlighting the refined elegance of the splendidly-preserved period furnishings.

there is a rose-window on the west wall and three windows on the east have led to speculation that this was originally the chapel of Haakon V's medieval castle. What is instead sadly certain is that after suffering serious damage in the fire of 1527, the hall became a warehouse for grain and other foodstuffs. Only in 1917, following philological research conducted by the architect Sinding-Larsen, the hall was restored and redesigned to the current floor plan and with the extraordinary ceilings, while sixty years later further work concentrated on the structure and decoration of the walls, taking as its model a medieval church, the Lårdal Stavkirke. It was then that the hall was dedicated to the reigning king, Olav V, who at the time was near to celebrating his 75th birthday.

But above and beyond these outstanding examples, the entire Castle is an extraordinary, gleaming coffer filled with treasures of art, history, and architecture, a precious jewel, every furthest and hidden corner surely meriting a visit.

IV Itinerary - Bygdøy

Dronningen - Kon-Tiki Museum - Fram Museum -
Norwegian Maritime Museum - Viking Ship Museum -
Norwegian Folk Museum

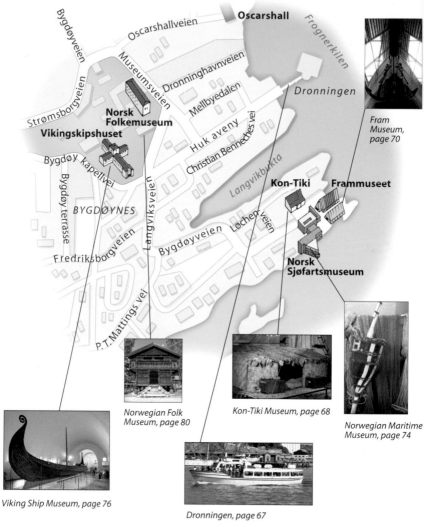

Fram
Museum,
page 70

Norwegian Folk
Museum, page 80

Kon-Tiki Museum, page 68

Norwegian Maritime
Museum, page 74

Viking Ship Museum, page 76

Dronningen, page 67

*Following the work carried out in the 1800s to fill in the strait that
separated it from the mainland, Bygdøy (literally, "inhabited island")
is now a lovely peninsula facing the center of Oslo, luxuriantly green,
covered in woodland and studded with typical cabins. A perfect place
to stroll in a luminous, relaxed atmosphere; to cycle, fish, swim in the
waters of the fjord, canoe, and sunbathe on uncontaminated beaches.
An attractive residential and recreational area that is always an
out-of-the ordinary destination for a day of relaxation, Bygdøy is also
a museum center, offering the occasion to visit some of Oslo's most
interesting, original exhibits.*

The ferries and other vessels that depart from the Port of Oslo for Bygdøy tie up at the jetty overshadowed by the modern profile of the peninsula's Dronningen.

DRONNINGEN

From Oslo's City Hall, ferries depart continually for the Bygdøy landing stage, which reaches out into the waters of the Oslofjord. Welcoming visitors to the peninsula is a building with sleek, essential lines, in Functionalist (Funkis) style, almost clinging to the jetty and facing the waters of the fjord: the Dronningen, a former very successful restaurant, inaugurated in the 1930s, that is now the headquarters of a popular sailing club.

KON-TIKI MUSEET
(Kon-Tiki Museum)

In 1947, with five companions and a large dose of courage, Thor Heyerdahl crossed the Pacific Ocean aboard an extremely lightweight raft,
the *Kon-Tiki*, covering 8,000 kilometers between Peru and Polynesia in
order to demonstrate that, in antiquity, the first Polynesians could have
come from South America. On Bygdøy, that raft and the papyrus boat
Ra II, on which Heyerdahl sailed from Morocco to the Barbados islands
in 1970 to demonstrate that ancient African mariners could well have
reached the Caribbean long before Columbus, are the centerpieces of an
interesting museum. Besides the vessels that starred in Heyerdahl's two
epic exploits, exhibits include objects and documents having to do with
the two voyages and also various finds brought back by Heyerdahl from
his expeditions, and in particular from Easter Island, as well as films,
slide shows, and the eighty thousand volumes of a library that boasts the
world's largest collection of works on the subject of Polynesia.

*Facing page, the Ra II, the papyrus boat
that in 1970 challenged the waters of the
Pacific Ocean for 57 days, with a crew
of eight, sailing 3270 miles from Safi, in
Morocco, to Barbados in the Caribbean.*

*The mythical Kon-Tiki, the balsa raft
on which, in 1947, Thor Heyerdahl
crossed the Pacific in 101 days,
from Peru to Polynesia, emerging
victorious from adventures of every
kind—not least, the threat of sharks.*

Kon-Tiki Museet

KON-TIKI
60th Anniversary
(1947-2007)

New exhibitions
and entertainment
for all ages at
The Kon-Tiki Museum
this year!

Kon-Tiki Museet

The unmistakable Frammuseet building, designed by the architect Bjarne Tøien and inaugurated on 20 May 1936, at the same time as the collections it houses, in the presence of King Haakon VII and Crown Prince Olav.

FRAMMUSEET
(Fram Museum)

In Bygdøy there's another museum, where every year 250,000 visitors flock to board the ship that sailed farther north and farther south than any other vessel in the world: the polar exploration vessel *Fram*. With the contribution of the Norwegian government, the ship was built in 1892 to plans by the Scotsman Colin Archer to permit Fridtjof Nansen to verify theories about the currents in the Arctic Ocean by drifting among the ice floes. For this reason it had to be small and light, but at the same time strong and of such a form that it would be lifted—and not crushed—by the pack ice. Thirty-nine meters in length with a five-meter draft, the *Fram* was the protagonist of three campaigns: the first under Nansen (1893-1896) and the second under Otto Sverdrup (1898-1902) were both

Frammuseet

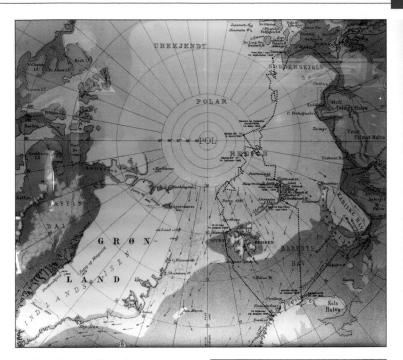

Maps of the expeditions, the sea routes, and the Arctic currents, utilitarian objects such as the skis and snowshoes used for traversing the ice, photographs documenting moments and situations that were often highly dramatic (left, the Fram *blocked by ice floes in January 1895): this is the epic world of the Frammuseet.*

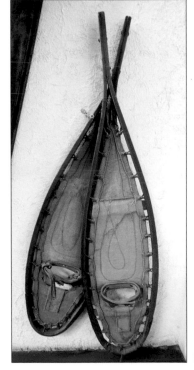

in the waters of the Arctic, toward the North Pole and Greenland; the third, in 1910-1912, took Roald Amundsen and his crew on four trips to the Arctic and Antarctica, where they planted the Norwegian flag at the South Pole. The expeditions were all undertaken in near-impossible conditions, with forced marches on skis and with sleds, tragedies caused by the cold and starvation, and even long months, in 1896, when the *Fram* was literally trapped in the ice. Upon her "retirement," the *Fram* was accurately restored and accorded a place of honor in the museum devoted to her exploits. Inaugurated in 1936, the declared aim of the museum is to keep alive the memory of the adventure and sacrifice that resulted in the conquest of the poles.

Frammuseet

71

The somewhat forbidding statue of the Fram's first skipper, Fridtjof Nansen, stands before the hull of the ship.

Frammuseet

Vessels of all types, from fishing boats to schooners, on display in a dedicated space, are among the main attractions at the Norwegian Maritime Museum, inaugurated in 1960.

Norsk Sjøfartsmuseum

NORSK SJØFARTSMUSEUM
(Norwegian Maritime Museum)

With its own landing-stage and looking south over the waters of the fjord, the Norwegian Maritime Museum offers a highly varied, detailed panorama of many different aspects of the Norwegian seagoing tradition, the flourishing, millenary fishing industry, and the renowned shipbuilding industry that has always been an essential part of the civilization and history of the country. The museum offers the visitor a key to a historical reading of the exhibits, with reconstructions of ships, fishing vessels, and whalers from various historical periods, and to analysis of the different ways in which man has related to the sea and organized his trade over the centuries. Dioramas, scale-models, objects recovered from shipwrecks and the polar expeditions, films, slide shows, documents of all kinds, and an interesting library pro-

Total mastery of the art of boat-building and the skills involved in designing and constructing excellent, incredibly strong hulls have always been the strong points of Norwegian industry and the country's unique relationship with the sea.

vide exhaustive evidence of the evolution of man's relationship with the coastal environment, while a marine archaeology center manages research projects and promotes protection of the finds come to light along Norway's coasts.

VIKINGSKIPSHUSET
(Viking Ship Museum)

One of the greatest chapters in Norwegian history is undoubtedly the glorious age of the Vikings, accomplished navigators who a thousand years ago sailed the world's sealanes for more than three centuries, reaching as far as the Americas; they were able merchants and courageous warriors supported by a civilization and a mindset that were highly advanced and at the avant-garde for the times. Today, three of their unmistakable ships (two in a perfect state of preservation and a third of which only several sections have come down to us) are the central exhibits at the "House of the Viking Ships," a building designed in 1914 by Arnstein Arneberg to provide an adequate

In the large photo and bottom, images of the Oseberg ship. Dating to the 9th century and recovered in 1904, it was perhaps designed to accompany the mortal remains of the Viking queen Åsa, who was buried together with a handmaiden and a rich array of possessions. The ship is 22 meters in length with 12 rows of planking, four less than the more or less coeval, 24-meter Gokstad ship, unearthed in 1880 (below left). In the inset, a detail of the elaborate decoration.

With its white facades and characteristic sloping roof, the Viking Ship Museum building was constructed with the express purpose of displaying the three great ships that were stored at temporary shelters at the University.

The Oseberg ship has come down to us essentially intact and thus offers a unique occasion to appreciate the details that set the Viking ships apart, like the elaborate decorations and the full complement of oars, which were shipped in special supports along the sides of the hull when not in use.

setting for these three extraordinary artifacts. The ships were discovered in three large burial mounds in the countryside in the Oslo fiord region. They are all vessels that were typically buried together with the deceased to carry the remains of illustrious figures, perhaps even members of the ruling families, on their last voyage to the kingdom of the dead. Together with the ships, the archaeologists also found the remains of men and women, as well as sleds, small boats, a wagon, jewels, utilitarian objects and tools, weapons. . . in short, true tomb furnishings, and even a funerary chamber in the form of a small wood cabin.

Buried for a thousand years under stone and clay, the ships were recovered with no small difficulty, even though the protection offered

Five finely-crafted zoomorphic heads were found on the Oseberg ship. While neither their significance nor their function is clear, they offer pregnant testimony to the levels of creative skill attained by the Viking craftsmen.

Vikingskipshuset

The Tune ship, the least well preserved of the three, dates to about 900 AD and was found in 1867. It was an oaken ship driven by a dozen rowers.

by the soil meant that two of them, the **Oseberg ship**, generally considered the most spectacular Viking vessel to have come down to us, and **Gokstad ship**, both named for the localities where they were found, reached the third millennium in what is generally considered a perfect state of preservation, leagues superior to any other similar find anywhere in the world. On the hull of the so-called **Tune ship**, on which the small funerary chamber was found, the long centuries of burial instead left indelible (and devastating) signs that it has been impossible to restore. Nevertheless, this ship offers precious information about Viking ship-building techniques, hull design, and the ships' extraordinary strength, which permitted them to cross even the oceans.

Another of the stylized animal heads from the Oseberg ship. The wealth of objects brought to light together with the ships offer a precious cutaway of customs and traditions at the time, but also of art and daily life in the era of the Vikings and their highly-evolved civilization.

Vikingskipshuset

Wooden farmhouses from various regions of the country, free-standing or arranged in groups around characteristic courts or threshing-floors, with stables, sheepcotes, storehouses, and other outbuildings, offer a concise cross-section of rural Norwegian civilization over the centuries.

NORSK FOLKEMUSEUM
(Norwegian Folk Museum)

What would you say to an open-air museum featuring 155 houses, typically rich in tradition, from the most disparate regions of Norway? Then the Norwegian Folk Museum is for you. Here, everything is lively and vibrant, from the activities for children to the guides, all dressed in brightly-colored local costumes, the many artisan workshops (where the characteristic wooden sculptures and other articles are crafted), and to horse-and-buggy rides and demonstrations of preparation of the typical *lefser*, a sort of sweet flat bread, and other dishes from Nor-

Norsk Folkemuseum

Young women in the typical dress of the various regions of Norway animate the ancient homes with their large family hearths. Top right, a service station, in concrete, dating to the 1920s and accurately restored with original fittings.

wegian cuisine. A visit to the enchanting Christmas Market is sure to remain etched in memory. Smaller exhibits illustrate traditional costumes, folk art, and Sami culture. A world apart, in short, which we owe to the creative enthusiasm and passion for folklore of Hans Aall, who in 1894, on the wings of patriotic fervor, decided to recreate the world

The spectacular wooden church from Gol. Perfectly preserved, it still contains precious statues and elegant decorations.

Norsk Folkemuseum

In the Norwegian Folk Museum you'll find perfect reconstructions of entire sections of cities; of particular note, a district of the ancient Christiania, with homes from other urban centers, recreating the Gamlebyen or "Old Town."

of the fjords and the farms, the fishermen, and big city life in a single location. All the buildings were fitted out with utilitarian objects and furnishings from the relative historic periods in order to provide detailed representations of the lifestyles of the rural and urban populations in different eras. But the most precious element among the many reproduced in this museum is undoubtedly the spectacular *Gol church* (12th-13th century), which was brought here in the late 1800s from Gol in the Hallingdal region. It is built entirely of wood in a marvelous, soaring, pagoda-like form.

Norsk Folkemuseum

Elegant reconstructions of interiors, furnishings in tasteful arrangements, the dreamy atmosphere of times past, and even galleries of sacred objects, statues, and paintings from churches from all over the country: this is the lively, fascinating world of the Norwegian Folk Museum.

Norsk Folkemuseum

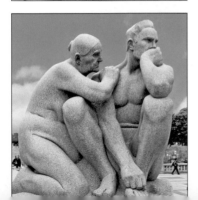

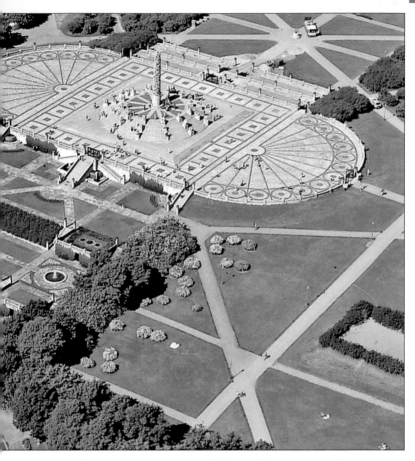

Images of Vigeland Park, showing several of the hundreds of sculptures created by Gustav Vigeland in granite, bronze, and wrought iron, representing man's sojourn on earth, in all its various phases, from the womb to death. Of particular note (bottom left) is the spectacular, 17-meter granite Monolith.

VIGELANDSPARKEN
(Vigeland Park)

Oslo's largest park is named for the great sculptor who devoted a great part of his life to it: Gustav Vigeland, who worked here from 1924 until his death in 1943 to create the 212 sculptural groups in bronze, granite, and wrought iron that illustrate the life and history of the human race in all its ages and forms. Vigeland was also the author of the parkland's layout and landscaping. Among the most spectacular pieces is the enormous *Monolith* at the summit of a staircase marked out by 36 granite groups representing the different ages in man's lifecycle. Seventeen meters in height, carved of a single block of granite, the *Monolith* is composed of 121 closely entwined figures straining toward the summit, which is actually reached only by a child. Every year, more than one million people visit the park, which is loved by tourists and the citizens of Oslo alike.

85

Open 24/24, the Vigelandsparken is universally renowned for its statues and the impressive Monolith (right) that rises at the summit of the lofty staircase, surrounded by 36 colossal granite sculpture groups. At the foot of the staircase, six giants support a fountain ringed by twenty bronze tree groups illustrating the four stages of life; sixty bas-reliefs, inspired by the same theme, line the lip of the fountain. But while we're on the subject of statues, all showing extraordinary dynamism and surprising expressiveness, we cannot but draw attention to the Sinnataggen, the famous "Angry Child" (below, right) that has by now become almost a symbol of Oslo.

HOLMENKOLLEN

Since 1892 the list of principal Norwegian attractions counts an impressive ski jump, the Holmenkollen. Today, it is 132.5 meters high, after having been modified and restructured many times over the decades. The Holmenkollen has been the venue for three world championships, the 1952 Olympic Games, and an indefinite number of popular contests in which even Crown Prince Olav participated in 1923 and 1924 when he was still heir-apparent to the Norwegian throne.

The modern-day Holmenkollen tower offers a splendid panorama of the capital and its fiord, while skiing down its jump is an absolutely unforgettable thrill. The Nordic ski arena all around offers other great sports facilities.

Since 1923, an interesting **museum** illustrating the history of skiing—an ancient tradition in Norway—and the evolution of the ski-based sports, the *Skimuseet*, has been located at the foot of the jump. Expanded in the late 20th century, the museum now also exhibits precious collections of works by Norwegian artists on the theme of skiing and boasts a section dedicated to the heroes of the polar expeditions.

On this and the following pages, breathtaking views of the ski jump on the Holmenkollen hill, a fabulously popular year-round attraction in Norway.

NORWAY AT THE TABLE

Custom dictates that Norwegians at home eat two main meals a day, breakfast—a hearty start to the day, with hot and cold fish and meat dishes, various processed meats, cakes, tarts, fruit in season, jam, and ginger and almond whole-grain cookies—and supper, usually an appetizer and a meat or fish entrée served with the ever-present potatoes and other vegetable side dishes (one specialty is mashed rutabaga, which is also used to make tasty dumplings), cow's and ewe's milk cheeses (like the delicious *geitost* and *brunost*), and fruit or dessert. The midday meal is frugal, simple but nutritious, a sort of cold buffet—the typical *koldtbord*—composed of meat and fish main courses accompanied by black bread and sauces, salads, and woodland fruits. In summer, **cold platters** of salami, sausages, ham, and dried or cured meats (*spekemat*) are worthy substitutes for the hot entrees and are served with sour cream, scrambled eggs, black bread, and *lefse*, a thin, crusty potato pancake about the consistency of a tortilla, made with potatoes.

Fish and Crustaceans
A peculiar style of cookery that owes much to tradition, Norway's, that has always fascinated visitors who want to learn more about the customs of the land of the fiords: a land bathed by uncontaminated seas, clear, ice-cold waters inhabited by a great variety of species of **fish** and the **crustaceans** and **mollusks** that are among the most typical ingredients of many Norwegian recipes. Not by chance, Norway is the "homeland" of the **cod**, a fish with compact, tasty flesh that the Vikings dried in the cold winds of their coasts and so created what later came to be

known worldwide as **stockfish** and is today an primary economic resource for the country. One of the best among the many recipes starring this fish (batter-fried, stewed, skewered and roasted, etc.) is *lutefisk*, stockfish soaked in lye water, skinned, boned, and boiled.

Another indisputable protagonist of the Norwegian board is **salmon**, smoked or fresh, cooked in infinite ways (boiled, cooked in various sauces, marinated, grilled) but especially delicate poached with vegetables and lemon slices, served with potatoes and cucumber salad. Other common fishes are **herring**, **catfish**, and **trout**, sometimes fermented (*rakfisk*) or used as an ingredient in rice croquettes. **Shellfish** are also popular dishes, fresh, smoked, salted, or marinated. **Crustaceans** (**shrimp** in particular) are ingredients in numerous, very popular and very tasty, traditional **fish-and-vegetable soups** and chowders.

Meats

But don't think for a minute that meat dishes are any less popular. Since ancient times, hunting has supplied excellent **game** for the table, while stock raising has always made available a variety of excellent meats, especially **pork**, **mutton**, and **lamb**. You'll also enjoy **moose**, **reindeer**, **venison**, and such wild fowl such as **duck** and **ptarmigian**. **Reindeer** and **moose**, in particular, are very popular; due to their strong gamey flavor, these meats are usually served with sour cream or special preserves, not overly sweet, generally made from woodland fruits.

Less exotic dishes that are nevertheless typically Norwegian are the **meat roll** (*rulle polse*), layered beef and pork rolled up with spices and simmered in water, and **meatballs** (ground beef, spices, and potato flour) in sauce. Other taste treats include

Eggs, cod and stockfish, the typical herrings, and the popular meatballs, meats of all kinds, and the ever-present salmon served with vegetables in season: from breakfast to supper, from antipastos to desserts, Norwegian cooking is closely linked to tradition—and for this reason a treasure chest of gustatory experience, all there for the tasting.

Cold platters accompanied by typical breads, thick vegetable and fish or crustacean soups, and meat entrées: all the recipes of Norwegian cooking are healthy and genuine, as one might expect from a people who since time immemorial have an intimate relationship with the sea and their land.

salted or smoked **lamb chops, lamb stewed** with cabbage, **pork meatballs** (*frikadeller*), **lamb ragout,** and **mutton stew.**

Breads

The perfect accompaniment to any entrée is **bread**, which the Norwegians make in many styles with wheat or barley and even potato flour. There are infinite varieties, from the soft sliced loaf to the almost unleavened *flatbrod*, from the aforementioned *lefse* to wholegrain bread and sweet rolls redolent with cinnamon. A special treat is the Norwegian Christmas bread, or *Julekake*, prepared in home kitchens during the Christmas season: light, delicious small loaves with dark and white raisins, cardamom, and candied fruit, decorated with candied cherries.

Norway's fish stews and entrées are simple but always tasty and filling dishes.

Drinks

As far as drinks go, local **beer** is excellent, usually pale, lager-style with a distinctive taste—but there are also many low-alcohol and even alcohol-free beers. A special sort of distilled liquor is also commonly served at the table: *akevitt*, made from fermented potatoes or grain, most often aromatized with caraway or fennel.

Woodland Fruits

And as a worthy conclusion to a Norwegian food festival, a precious gift of Nature in this land with its often harsh northern climate: the sweet **woodland fruits**, used for making desserts and confectionery but also the preserves that accompany meat entrées. Wild or cultivated, Norway produces **cranberries** and **blueberries**, **raspberries**, **strawberries**, **currants**, and **gooseberries**, but the most divine of the Norwegian woodland fruits is certainly the **cloudberry** (*multer*), the fruit of a wild plant that thrives only at the northern latitudes.

INDEX